I0814277

DISCOVERING THE UNITED STATES

Tennessee

BY LIZ SONNEBORN

An Imprint of Abdo Publishing
abdobooks.com

abdobooks.com

Printed in China.
052024
092024

Cover Photo: iStockphoto
Interior Photos: Shutterstock Images, 4–5, 15, 22, 26; Steve Byland/Shutterstock Images, 7 (top left); Jon Benedictus/Shutterstock Images, 7 (top right); iStockphoto, 7 (bottom left); Damon Herota/iStockphoto, 7 (bottom right); Mark Van Dyke Photography/Shutterstock Images, 9; Marcus E. Jones/Shutterstock Images, 10; Matt Hamilton/Chattanooga Times Free Press/AP Images, 12–13; Casey Flanigan/Imagespace/Alamy Live News/Alamy, 16; Gary Miller/Getty Images Entertainment/Getty Images, 18; Kevin Ruck/Shutterstock Images, 20–21; Sean Pavone/Shutterstock Images, 24, 29 (bottom); Red Line Editorial, 28 (top), 29 (middle); Jim Vallee/Shutterstock Images, 28 (bottom); Joseph Hendrickson/Shutterstock Images, 29 (top)

Editor: Christa Kelly
Series Designer: Katharine Hale

Library of Congress Control Number: 2023949337

Publisher's Cataloging-in-Publication Data

Names: Sonneborn, Liz, author.
Title: Tennessee / by Liz Sonneborn
Description: Minneapolis, Minnesota: Abdo Publishing, 2025 | Series: Discovering the United States | Includes online resources and index.
Identifiers: ISBN 9781098294137 (lib. bdg.) | ISBN 9798384913405 (ebook)
Subjects: LCSH: U.S. states--Juvenile literature. | Tennessee--History--Juvenile literature. | Southeastern States--Juvenile literature. | Physical geography--United States--Juvenile literature.
Classification: DDC 973--dc23

All population data taken from:
"Estimates of Population by Sex, Race, and Hispanic Origin: April 1, 2020 to July 1, 2022." *US Census Bureau, Population Division,* June 2023, census.gov.

CONTENTS

Musicians perform more than 6,000 songs at the Grand Ole Opry every year.

The Grand Ole Opry

"Have a big time tonight," country star Roy Acuff sang. It was October 14, 1939. Crowds were gathered at the Grand Ole Opry in Nashville, Tennessee.

The Opry is a show famous for its country music. That night, big stars were performing.

People at home listened to the show over the radio. It was the first Opry show **broadcast** to much of the country. The audience loved it.

The Opry has been on the radio ever since. It made country music popular across the United States. It also made Nashville an important part of the music **industry**. Nashville is now known as Music City.

Tennessee's Land

Tennessee is in the South region of the United States. Kentucky and Virginia border it to the north. To the east is North Carolina. Georgia, Alabama, and Mississippi are to the south. To the west lies the Mississippi River. It separates the state from Arkansas and Missouri.

Tennessee Facts

DATE OF STATEHOOD
June 1, 1796

CAPITAL
Nashville

POPULATION
7,051,339

AREA
42,144 square miles
(109,153 sq km)

STATE BIRD

Mockingbird

STATE TREE

Tulip poplar

STATE FLOWER

Passion flower

STATE MAMMAL

Raccoon

Each US state has a different population, size, and capital city. States also have state symbols.

Tennessee has several different **terrains**.

East Tennessee has the Unaka Mountains.

Middle Tennessee has rolling hills and valleys.

In West Tennessee, the terrain is flatter. Swamps are found near the Mississippi River.

Forests cover about half of Tennessee. They are home to white-tailed deer, beavers, and rabbits. Black bears and wild hogs live in the mountains.

Tennessee has many rivers. The Tennessee River curves along its eastern and western borders. The Cumberland River cuts through northern Tennessee.

Tennessee National Wildlife Refuge

The Tennessee National Wildlife **Refuge** is near Kentucky Lake in northwestern Tennessee. It stretches across more than 51,000 acres (21,000 ha). The refuge is home to more than 300 types of birds.

The Unaka Mountains separate Tennessee and North Carolina.

The state also has many lakes. About half were made by humans. This includes Tennessee's biggest lake, Kentucky Lake.

The Tennessee River is home to at least 230 species of fish.

Tennessee has long, hot summers. Leaves turn red, orange, and yellow in the fall. Winters are short and mild. East Tennessee has the coldest temperatures. This region also gets the most snow. In the spring, the weather warms and flowers bloom.

Explore Online

Visit the website below. Does it give any new information about the Grand Ole Opry that wasn't in Chapter One?

Grand Ole Opry

abdocorelibrary.com/discovering-tennessee

The Cherokee Nation is the largest American Indian nation in the United States.

The People of Tennessee

The first people in Tennessee were American Indians. For thousands of years, the land was home to the Cherokee and the Chickasaw nations. The Cherokee lived in the east. In the west were the Chickasaw. Both nations farmed and hunted.

Europeans first arrived in Tennessee in 1540. They were looking for gold. In the late 1600s, white **settlers** began moving onto the land. Some brought enslaved Black people to the region and forced them to work on farms.

As the Europeans took more and more land, tensions rose between settlers and American Indians. In the 1830s, the US government forced American Indians to

The Volunteer State

Thousands of people from Tennessee volunteered to fight in the War of 1812 (1812–1815). Soldiers from other states were impressed by their spirit. Thousands more volunteered during the Mexican-American War (1846–1848). This earned Tennessee the nickname the Volunteer State.

Tennessee's current flag was adopted in 1905.

leave Tennessee and move west. They had to walk most of the way. The journey took more than six months. Many died. Some were separated from their families. This removal is known as the Trail of Tears.

Today, only about 0.5 percent of people in Tennessee are American Indian. Almost 73 percent are white. Nearly 17 percent are Black. About 6 percent are Hispanic or Latino, and 2 percent are Asian.

Taylor Swift lived in Hendersonville, Tennessee.

Culture

Sports are important to people in Tennessee. Football fans cheer on the Titans. Basketball fans root for the Memphis Grizzlies. Hockey fans cheer for the Nashville Predators.

Food is another important part of Tennessee culture. Nashville is known for its spicy chicken. Many people also love barbeque and salty ham. Cornbread is a popular side dish.

Tennessee is famous for its music. Many music genres began in Tennessee, including blues, country, gospel, soul, and rock and roll. Many singers are also from Tennessee. Singer and actress Miley Cyrus was born in the state. Pop star Taylor Swift moved to Tennessee at age 13 to begin her music career.

Industries

Entertainment is one of Tennessee's biggest industries. Some people make movies and TV shows. Other people work in music.

Tennessee hosts more than a dozen music festivals every year.

Some perform. Others write songs or build instruments. Tennessee's music industry brings in $5.8 billion every year.

Farming is another important industry in Tennessee. The state's farmers grow many crops, including corn, cotton, and soybeans. Farmers there also raise cattle and chickens.

Other people in the state work in **manufacturing**. Some make technology. They build cars and computers. Others make food and beverages.

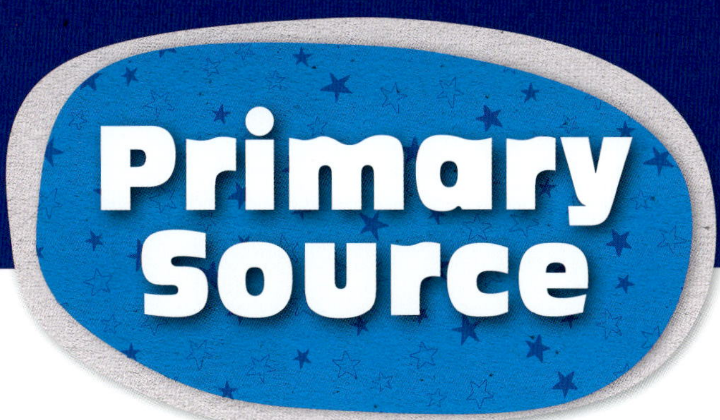

Singer Tina Turner spent her childhood in a small town in Tennessee. In her book *My Love Story*, she wrote:

> I wouldn't change a thing. . . . We were part of a lively community of family and friends. Everyone worked hard, played hard, and worshipped at church on Sunday.

Source: Tina Turner, with Deborah Davis and Dominik Wichmann. *My Love Story*. Atria, 2018, p. 26.

What's the Big Idea?

Read the quote carefully. What is its main idea? Explain this idea in a few sentences.

In 1843, Nashville became the capital of Tennessee.

Places in Tennessee

Nashville is the capital of Tennessee. It is also the state's most **populated** city. Nashville is located in central Tennessee.

Millions of tourists travel to Nashville every year. Many come to learn about the city's role in shaping the music industry.

The Country Music Hall of Fame and Museum opened in 1967.

One of the city's most famous sites is the Country Music Hall of Fame and Museum.

Memphis is the second most populated city in Tennessee. It is located in the southwestern corner of the state. People come to Memphis to see Graceland. This is the mansion where rock and roll star Elvis Presley used to live.

The mansion has been turned into a museum to teach people about the singer.

Memphis is also home to the National Civil Rights Museum. The museum teaches visitors about the history of racism in the United States. It also highlights the Black leaders who fought for equal rights. The museum is located in the motel where civil rights leader Martin Luther King Jr. was **assassinated**.

Parks

Tennessee has many beautiful parks. The most famous is Great Smoky Mountains National Park. With 10 million yearly visitors, it is the most popular national park in the country. People come to see the park's natural beauty.

Great Smoky Mountains National Park is located on the border of Tennessee and North Carolina.

The park has many mountains and rivers. It is home to deer, elk, and black bears.

Tennessee also has many state parks. One of the most popular is Rock Island State Park in central Tennessee. Its scenic hiking trails lead to massive waterfalls. The park is also home to a historic fabric factory. The factory used one of the waterfalls to power its machines.

Landmarks

Lookout Mountain is located in southern Tennessee. It overlooks Chattanooga. The mountain is 2,000 feet (600 m) tall.

Dollywood

Just miles from Great Smoky Mountains National Park is a popular amusement park. The park is called Dollywood. It is named after famous country music singer Dolly Parton. She opened the park in the 1980s. It is near Sevierville, Parton's hometown. The park attracts millions of visitors each year.

An explorer discovered the underground waterfall in 1928 and named it after his wife, Ruby.

Inside the mountain is Ruby Falls, the tallest underground waterfall in the country. Visitors can take a glass elevator down into the mountain to see the waterfall.

The Grand Ole Opry House is one of Tennessee's most famous landmarks. The Opry was founded in 1925 to showcase country music. Today, the Opry plays all kinds of music. It holds shows every week. Each show features eight or more musicians. The theater moved into its current building in 1974. It can hold more than 4,300 people.

Tennessee has something for everyone. The state has amazing food, breathtaking views, and a fascinating history. From music to scenic waterfalls, Tennessee is a land of beauty.

Further Evidence

Look at the website below. Does it give any new evidence to support Chapter Three?

Nashville

abdocorelibrary.com/discovering-tennessee

State Map

KEY

Point of interest

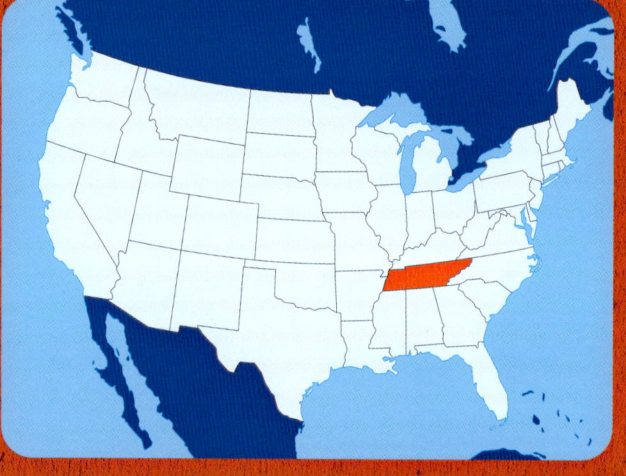

Rock Island State Park

Dollywood

Tennessee: The Volunteer State

Memphis

Glossary

assassinated
murdered for political reasons

broadcast
to send out information, often on radio, television, or the internet

industry
a group of businesses that serve similar purposes

manufacturing
the process of making goods to sell

populated
settled or lived in

refuge
a sheltered or protected place

settlers
people who moved to a new area

terrain
the features of an area of land

Online Resources

To learn more about Tennessee, visit our free resource websites below.

Visit **abdocorelibrary.com** or scan this QR code for free Common Core resources for teachers and students, including vetted activities, multimedia, and booklinks, for deeper subject comprehension.

Visit **abdobooklinks.com** or scan this QR code for free additional online weblinks for further learning. These links are routinely monitored and updated to provide the most current information available.

Learn More

Bird, F. A. *Cherokee.* Abdo, 2022.

Loggia, Wendy. *Taylor Swift.* Golden Books, 2023.

Tieck, Sarah. *Tennessee.* Abdo, 2020.

Index

About the Author

Liz Sonneborn is the author of more than 100 books for young readers. She specializes in American history, world history, biography, American Indian studies, and women's history. Now a resident of Brooklyn, New York, Sonneborn spent her teenage years in Nashville, Tennessee. She still visits family and friends in the city.